Flowers of
Zion National Park

This book was created to celebrate the flowers of Zion NP. Each coloring page will come with a color guide (but color the pictures however you want, you do you).

Along with when and where to find these beauties.
Plus a bonus fun fact about the plant.
Enjoy coloring your way through Zion with this book.

Thank you!

Sacred Datura

When it blooms: April-June

Where to see it: Lower Zion Canyon

Flower Facts: These flowers are also called moon flowers, since they open up at night and close in the morning.

Color Profile: White flower with deep green leaves

Zion Shootingstar

When it blooms: May-August

Where to see it: Hanging gardens along Riverside Walk, Weeping Rock, and Emerald Pools trails

Flower Facts: This plant thrives in wet areas and is easily found in the hanging gardens of Zion.

Color profile: Pale Purple with yellow centers and deep maroon stigmas

Columbine

When it blooms: May-August

Where to see it: Weeping Rock, Emerald Pools, and Riverside Walk trails

Flower Facts: Columbine comes from the Latin for "dove", due to the resemblance of the inverted flowers posing as five doves clustered together.

Color Profile: Bright Red petals turning yellow towards the center

Spotted Fritillary

When it blooms: April-June

Where to see it: Shady forested areas

Flower Facts: This flower is also called the Checker Lily, which it's easy to see why it got that nickname

Color Profile: Yellow with dark red "spots"

Globe Mallow

When it blooms: June-August

Where to see it: Dry, sunny slopes in the park

Flower Facts: This plant has been used medicinally for hundreds of years by Native Americans.

Color Profile: Bright Orange

Zion Draba

When it blooms: March–April

Where to see it: East Rim Trail, Checkboard Mesa

Flower Facts: Notice the name? Yup, that's because this specific species of flower only exists within Utah.

Color Profile: Bright Yellow

Golden Columbine

When it blooms: July-October

Where to see it: Hanging gardens along Riverside Walk, Weeping Rock, and Emerald Pools trails

Flower Facts: This plant thrives in wet areas and is easily found in the hanging gardens of Zion.

Color Profile: Bright Yellow

Yucca

When it blooms: April-June

Where to see it: Throughout the park

Flower Facts: 5 species of Yucca exist in Zion
and all 5 are pollinated by only one species,
the yucca moth.

Color Profile: White to pale pink

Manzanita

When it blooms: February-March

Where to see it: Edges of canyon walls and on the sides of steep sandstone cliffs

Flower Facts: Manzanita means "little apple" and the name describes the tiny, apple-like fruit.

Color Profile: White to pale purple

Wood's Rose

When it blooms: April-June

Where to see it: Canyon and Plateau areas

Flower Facts: This plant's berries are an important food source for the mule deer in the winter.

Color Profile: Bight Pink

Ashy Silk-Tassel

When it blooms: January to April

Where to see it: Washes & canyons

Flower Facts: This shrub is an vital food source for the mule deer during the winter months.

Color Profile: Light green with touches of purple

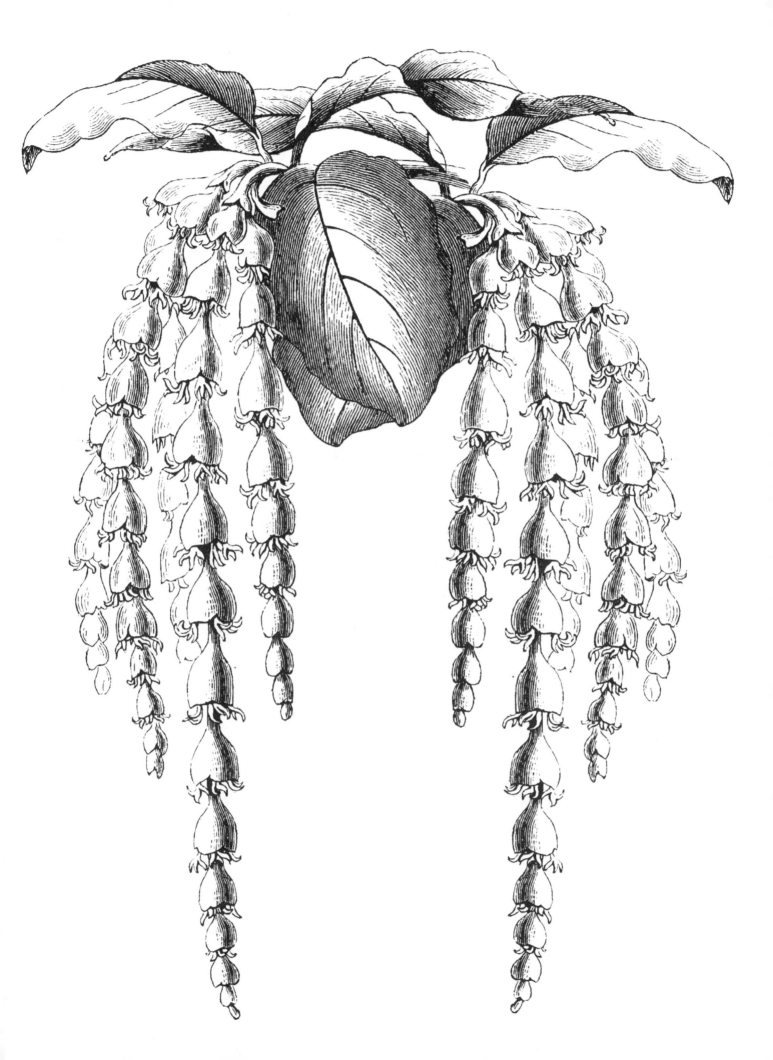

Prickly Pear Cactus

When it blooms: May-June

Where to see it: Throughout the park

Flower Facts: The fruit from these cactus are very tasty and people often make jam and other sweets with them.

Color Profile: Yellow or Pink

Wild Rhubarb

When it blooms: January- May

Where to see it: Canyons and Wash Areas

Flower Facts: This plant has been used for centuries by the Native Americans. The roots are used to make tannin to dye leathers and the leaves and stalks cooked for food.

Color Profile: Dark Pink

Crimson Monkeyflower

When it blooms: May - September

Where to see it: Riverside Walk Trail, Canyon areas

Flower Facts: Look closely and you might spot the "monkey" face that gives the plant its name.

Color Profile: Dark Red

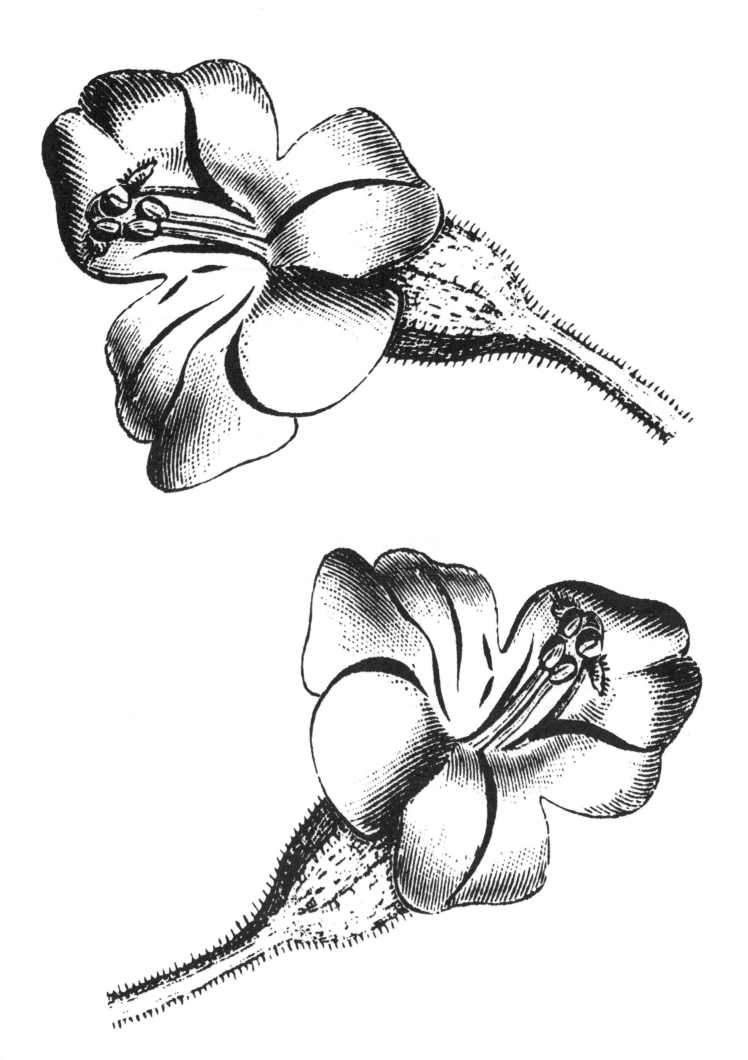

Hummingbird flower

When it blooms: July-November

Where to see it: Throughout the park

Flower Facts: These shrub with it's abundance of flowers is a critical food source for native bees and migrating hummingbirds

Color Profile: Bright Red

Wild Blue Flax

When it blooms: March-September

Where to see it: Canyon and wash areas.

Flower Facts: This plant has bother medicinal and practical uses. Native Americans have used the stems and leaves to make teas to help with eye and stomach problems. They also used the stems to make strong rope.

Color Profile: Pale Blue

Colorado Four O'clock

When it blooms: April-September

Where to see it: Dry slopes and mesas

Flower Facts: Blooming only when shaded
and at twilight , these flowers are a favorite
food of the native Hawk Moth

Color Profile: Deep Pink

Miner's lettuce

When it blooms: February-May

Where to see it: Hanging Gardens and Riparian areas

Flower Facts: This plant preferes cool wet places.

Color Profile: Pink or white

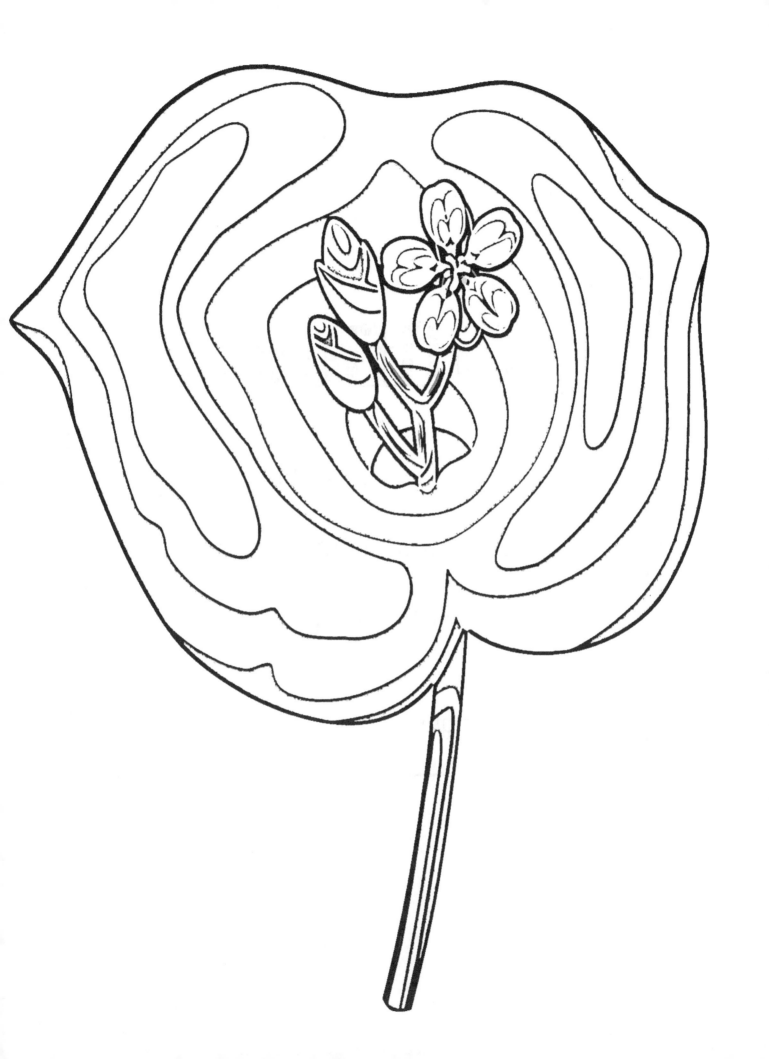

Wallflower

When it blooms: July-September

Where to see it: Throughout the park

Flower Facts: This flower is part of the mustard family.

Color Profile: Bright Yellow

Hooker's Onion

When it blooms: June-July

Where to see it: Canyons and Plateaus

Flower Facts: Every part of this plant is edible, including the flower.

Color Profile: Purple

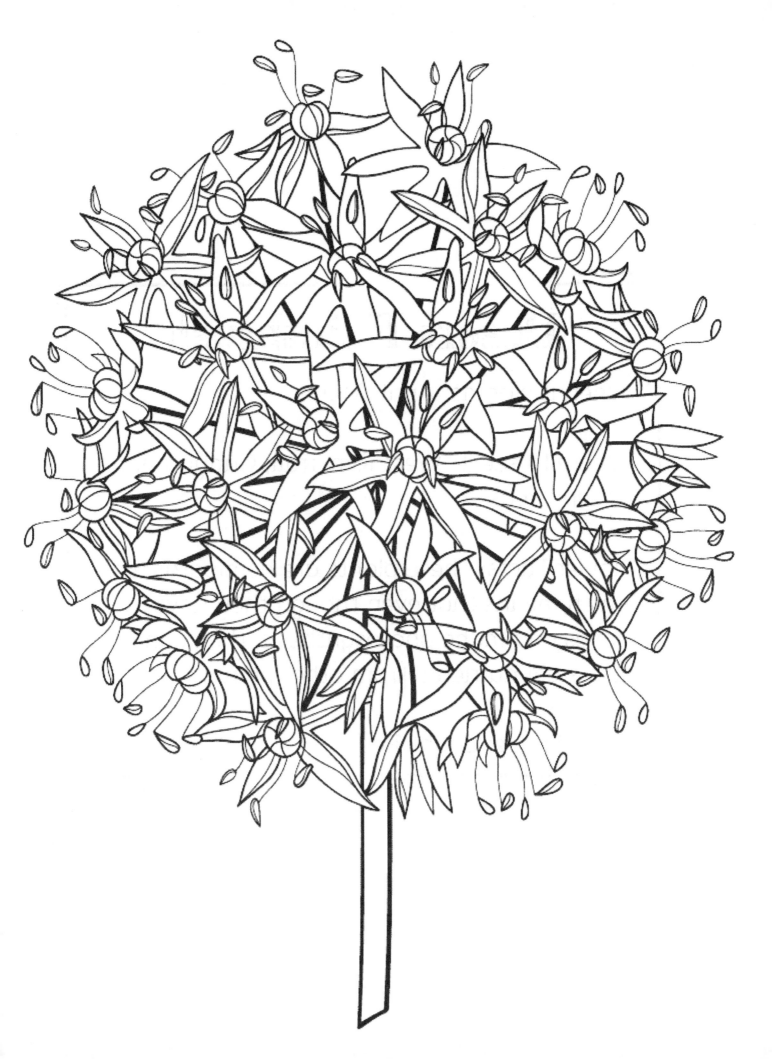

Desert Paintbrush

When it blooms: April-May

Where to see it: West Rim Trail, Canyon and Desert areas

Flower Facts: These plants are hemiparasites, which means that even though they have leaves and make photosynthesis, they can also steal nutrients from other plants.

Color Profile: Bright Red

Desert Marigold

When it blooms: March–November

Where to see it: Desert Areas of the Park

Flower Facts: Dense patches often form solid strips of yellow along miles of desert roadsides.

Color Profile: Bright Yellow

Hedgehog Cactus

When it blooms: April

Where to see it: Lower Zion Canyon,
Desert Areas

Flower Facts: This cactus got it's common
name from the spiny and edible fruit it
produces.

Color Profile: Pale Pink **to Bright Red**

Zion milkvetch

When it blooms: April-June

Where to see it: Pa-rus Trail, ,Canyon Areas

Flower Facts: Another plant only existing in the Utah and Zion area, this plant is one of the first to bloom in the spring.

Color Profile: Purple

Fleabane

When it blooms: July-October

Where to see it: Throughout the Park

Flower Facts: There are close to 400 species of Fleabane. 9 exist within the park including the Zion Daisy.

Color Profile: White to dark blue

Yarrow

When it blooms: March-October

Where to see it: Canyon and Plateau areas

Flower Facts: Yarrow is so wide spread that it is found in many countries histories and folklore.

Color Profile: This flowers come in every color imaginable. So let your imagine run wild.

Water Speedwell

When it blooms: March-November

Where to see it: Moist meadows and streambanks

Flower Facts: This plant is semi-aquatic so look for it near slow moving water.

Color Profile: Pale purple

Common Mullein

When it blooms: June-August

Where to see it: Flat grassy areas

Flower Facts: Though not native to the US, this plant is impressive in it's ability to grow up to 6 feet tall.

Color profile: Yellow

Larkspur

When it blooms: April-August

Where to see it: Throughout the park

Flower Facts: Though this flower comes in many different colors, the 3 varieties inside the park are all purple or blue.

Color profile: Dark purple or Blue

Chicory

When it blooms: March-October

Where to see it: Grassland, roadsides; moist areas

Flower Facts: Chicory originates in Europe, and is grown for its edible roots and leaves; the main use is as a coffee substitute.

Color profile: Bright Blue

Indian Hyacinth

When it blooms: Year around

Where to see it: Canyon and Plateau areas

Flower Facts: This plant can stay dormant for many years and likes to appear after fire has occurred in it's area.

Color profile: Light Purple

Lupine

When it blooms: April-June

Where to see it: Washes and sandy areas

Flower Facts: Lupine means "wolf" in Latin. These flowers were named this because it was once thought that they sucked too many nutrients from the soil, when in fact the opposite is true, and these plants fix nitrogen to the soil and are beneficial to other plants.

Color profile: Blue and Purple

Russian Thistle

When it blooms: July - September

Where to see it: Roadsides

Flower Facts: While 5 feet is more common, this plant can grow up to 8 feet tall. This is a non-native plant.

Color profile: Dark purple

Stiff Gentian

When it blooms: August-October

Where to see it: Woodland borders, streambanks and roadbanks

Flower Facts: Another medicinal plant, the root has been used as a cure for intestinal worms and fevers.

Color profile: Light to dark purple

Monkey Flower

When it blooms: May-October

Where to see it: Streambanks, seeps, springs, canyon alcoves

Flower Facts: The flowers of some species are said to resemble a monkey's face.

Color profile: Yellow, Orange or Red

Horsemint Giant Hyssop

When it blooms: June-August

Where to see it: Meadows and riparian areas.

Flower Facts: This plant can get up to 3 feet tall.

Color profile: Purple

Mountain Dandelion

When it blooms: June-August

Where to see it: Plateau areas

Flower Facts: This plant was used by Native Americans for medicinal uses such as an external pain-relieving liniment for sprains, fractures, and bruising.

Color profile: Orange

Mountain Phlox

When it blooms: April-June

Where to see it: Scrubland, forests, mountain slopes

Flower Facts: There are 5 native pholx species within Zion.

Color profile: Pale to deep blue